PESTS

BLACK'S PICTURE INFORMATION BOOKS

Scientific Adviser Jean Imrie M Sc

pests

MATTHEW PRIOR

Adam and Charles Black · London

Published by A & C Black Ltd
4, 5 & 6 Soho Square, London WIV 6AD

First published 1973 Reprinted 1975

ISBN 0 7136 1317 3

First published in the Netherlands by Moussault's Uitgeverij NV under the title *Schadelijke en lastige dieren* with a text by J C Niesthoven; this text translated by Adrienne Dixon and adapted by Matthew Prior with the assistance of Jean Imrie.

Filmset by Photoprint Plates Ltd, Rayleigh, Essex
Printed in the Netherlands by Ysel Press, Deventer

Acknowledgements

The publishers and author are grateful to the following for their permission to reproduce illustrations:

Colour: V-Dia Verlag pages 19, 20, 22, 23, 24, 25, 27, 30, 31, 32, 34, 36, 38; Polyvisie NV page 35; Luctor NV pages 35, 37, 39; J C Niesthoven pages 18, 19, 20, 21, 26, 27, 28, 29, 30, 31, 33, 35, 37, 38, 39.

Black and white: Mansell Collection pages 9, 11; Mary Evans Picture Library pages 6, 45, 49, 53; L Hugh Newman page 51; J C Niesthoven pages 18, 40, 41; Parool Archive page 17; Radio Times Hulton Picture Library page 43.

Contents

A rat-catcher of about 1600

People live in houses for warmth and shelter. Mice, beetles, cockroaches and flies enter our houses because they too are looking for shelter, and also for food. People provide both. The food may be our own, found in pantries and larders, or it may be something else—clothes, soap, even the paste behind the wallpaper. In the case of lice and fleas part of the food is us.

In the wild these same creatures are not 'pests' at all. It is only when they are in our buildings (schools, warehouses, and factories as well as homes) that we call them 'pests', and often it is only when they are present in large numbers that we worry about them.

Some people are ashamed to admit it when they suddenly find they have mice. Others are scared stiff of 'creepy-crawlies', or of rodents. But if we are to get rid of the harmful animals, the best way to start is by studying their habits. Then we can use our knowledge in the fight against them.

We certainly need to protect our health and property against pests, but we also need to think first about what we are doing. You will discover in this book that some 'pests' are in the long run useful to us. If we eliminate whole species, it may have surprising results—and it is almost certain that another 'pest' will take over from the one we have destroyed.

This book will help you identify some common creatures which many people would like to pretend do not exist. You will be able to decide how harmful (or otherwise) the creature is, and will find out how to get rid of it if necessary.

The damage done by pests

Some history

Insects first appeared on earth many millions of years ago. Since man evolved only about one million years ago, we can assume that both he and his ape-like ancestors were plagued by pests from the very beginning.

There are some true human parasites, such as fleas and lice, but early man must have also had to protect the meat he had hunted from voracious rats, mice and beetles.

Later, when man had learned to cultivate crops, great plagues developed, such as the plagues of frogs, flies (probably tsetse flies) and lice which 'punished' the Egyptians in the Bible.

Rats and mice also caused great misery. When the Bible says: 'That night the angel of the Lord went out, and smote in the camp of the Assyrians a hundred, four score and five thousand', the number is exaggerated, but the bubonic plague had probably arrived in the camp. This plague is carried by the fleas of the black rat.

Throughout history, military campaigns were more often ended by disease than by battle. Henry V's army was very nearly destroyed before the battle of Agincourt by 'camp fever' or dysentry (a disease transmitted by flies) and Henry himself died of the disease a few years later.

A mouse shown in a Roman mosaic

Sometimes the results were less dramatic. On the morning of 27 June 1816, the ex-emperor Napoleon, in exile on the island of St Helena, was unable to have breakfast because the rats had eaten everything.

The fight against pests started early. Rat-catchers were to be found in London in the fourteenth century. In later centuries they were to develop a cunning trick; they did not kill the rats they caught, but took them to another place, and released them. In this way they were able to catch the same rats several times over.

The damage done by pests

The damage which mankind suffers from animals throughout the world is caused by less than 1% of animal species. Most animals are either harmless or useful to us.

What is a pest? What is a harmful animal? These questions are not easy to answer, because what one person may find harmful or troublesome is not so to another. Let us start by considering the damage done. There are several kinds of damage:

    Damage to health
    Damage to houses and buildings
    Damage to food
    Damage to clothing and other property
    Damage to plants

Damage to health

The damage which some animals can do to health is due to various poisonous substances in their bodies which, when secreted or injected, have a harmful effect on man or animals. In the case of insect bites or stings, the effect is usually limited to one part of our body, but in some cases (plague, malaria, etc) the effect is more general and more serious.

We could all agree that a rat flea is a danger to human health, because it spreads plague, but what about the ordinary gnat?

Is it harmful or only troublesome? Some people, when bitten, only feel a slight itch, but others are allergic to gnat poison, and can suffer great discomfort as a result of a bite. And if we are kept awake by a mosquito buzzing round our bedroom, we might say that the lack of sleep will affect our health!

In temperate countries we do not suffer much from creatures which carry dangerous diseases, but in tropical countries such animals can be a real menace. Besides the rat flea which carries bubonic plague (of which the last known in Britain was in 1910) and also a form of typhus called 'jail fever', there are the body louse which can transmit typhus fever, the malaria mosquito which can transmit malaria, and the tsetse fly which transmits sleeping sickness.

Our main problems in temperate countries are with bites and stings, and damage is usually restricted to:

a. Inflammation. Sometimes there is also a slight rise in temperature. Caused by the stings and bites of bees, wasps, bedbugs, lice or mosquitoes.

Accidit anno predicto q in die Assumptionis virginis gloriose venerunt a villa brugen si araiter .cc. hominibus: quasi hora ceperunt compati personis et penitentie condolere et deo gra tias reddere super tanta peni tentia quam gravissimam re

During the Black Death some people thought that the plague was a punishment sent by God. They went from town to town beating themselves, hoping that as a result God would forgive them. These people were called flagellants

b. Painful stings. Sometimes the sting hurts and that is all, but sometimes it goes on itching for a time. Caused by bees, wasps and ants.
c. Itching swellings. These are usually round whitish patches which itch for some time after the bite. Caused by bedbugs and mosquitoes.
d. Little lumps. These are usually red and do not always itch. Caused by fleas, horse-flies, ticks and stable flies.
e. Skin rash. Usually there is severe itching as well. Caused by lice, mites, and the irritating hairs of some kinds of caterpillar.

Some creatures appear in more than one category because they have different effects on different people.

It is worth remembering the treatment for various common stings and bites. For *bee stings*, apply bicarbonate of soda to the skin. For *wasp stings*, apply vinegar or lemon juice. Many people are allergic to wasp stings and the area around the sting may swell alarmingly. If you are allergic, it is worth asking a doctor or chemist for suitable antihistamine tablets. If you are stung in the mouth, go to a doctor immediately, because swelling in the throat can make it hard to breathe.

The treatment for a rash caused by a cater-pillar is to apply olive oil or vinegar.

Damage to houses and buildings

In tropical countries, termites can ruin houses by eating the woodwork. They also eat books. We have no termites in Britain but we have other pests which do the same things, though more slowly.

Woodworm, for example, is not a worm at all, but the larva of a tiny beetle. It can eat its way through furniture and other wood. There are other beetle larvae which can destroy furniture, floorboards or rafters in a few years.

Rats cause quite extensive damage by gnawing and digging, and the damage they cause is often expensive to repair.

Damage to food

Most households do not have large stocks of food, so the loss of food because of pests in houses or large kitchens is not great; but all the same, there are a number of animals we would rather be without. Rats and mice, for example, nibble our food, and also soil it with their droppings.

Cockroaches are less well known, because they only come out in the dark. They can be found even in modern kitchens, especially in institutions such as schools or hospitals.

Other animals—usually small creatures—gorge themselves on cereals. Examples are the bread-beetle, flour mite and mealworm, as well as weevils and a species of ant known as Pharaoh's ant.

Damage to clothing and other property

Few people would say that moths are not pests, but of course the adult moth does no damage at all to clothes. The damage is done by the larvae of the moth, which cause extensive damage. Obviously the adult moth has to be destroyed too.

Apart from rats and mice which will readily eat clothing, it is almost always insect larvae which cause this kind of damage. The larvae of the carpet moth and fur beetle cause even more destruction than the clothes moth. They usually prefer animal fibres (especially wool) but will sometimes even eat nylon!

Damage to plants

Most damage to plants occurs on farms, and in this book we shall only mention a few garden pests, such as slugs, earwigs, ants and aphids. In semi-tropical countries the locust causes immense damage to crops.

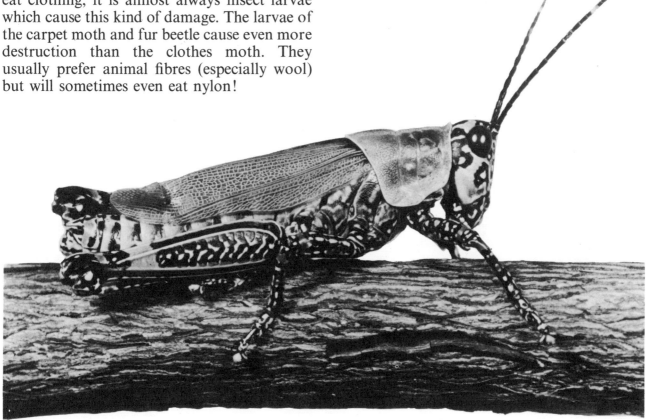

The locust. This species of grasshopper travels in great swarms, which may completely destroy any crop on which they land

The rabbit—a pet if you decide to keep it as a pet, but certainly a pest in the eyes of farmers

The place of 'pests' in nature

There is no such thing as a 'harmful' animal in nature. Every animal has its place. What we mean by a pest is an animal which is harmful *to man*.

Usually people attract pests to themselves by providing a source of food or shelter for the pests. For example, if people were more careful about personal hygiene—washing themselves, their clothes and their bedclothes more often —there would be fewer fleas and lice. If people were more careful with their leftovers after meals, rats and mice would stay in the fields and we would have no food-eating insects in the house. And if people took the obvious precautions when having a house built, no rats or mice would ever get into the building.

Rats and mice don't slip past when you open the front door. In many cases they come in through a gap left where a pipe goes through an outside wall. In nine cases out of ten the hole hacked through the wall is considerably larger than the pipe, and usually it is badly sealed afterwards. So the new house allows easy access for rodents.

Most of these animals need little food to stay alive and to reproduce, and man supplies it.

In the natural state these animals fulfil a useful role, and it is man's civilisation which has enticed them into being pests.

The 'uses' of harmful animals

What are the useful roles that these pests fulfil in their natural state?

Sometimes their destructiveness is very useful. For example, every day people die in all our towns and cities, and we arrange for their bodies to be buried or cremated. Many other living creatures die each day—millions of dead animals and plants, varying in size from microscopic plants to dead cows and sheep in the fields.

These dead bodies could easily spread disease as they rot, but normally they are cleared away by other animals which eat dead meat, and among these animals are quite a few which we would call 'pests'.

Rats eat a large number of dead animals. Moths lay their eggs in the fur of a dead animal and their larvae eat the fur. Many beetles and flies lay their eggs on carcasses, and the larvae eat the carcass. Cockroaches, slugs and earwigs feed on dead plant matter.

Even the animals which spread diseases are doing a service, by making sure that no one species can become too numerous. Man too has been controlled by disease although now medicine has done much to eliminate such diseases, and in the process has created problems of over-population!

Should we kill animals which are harmful?

Since so many of the animals which we call pests do in fact fulfil a useful role, the answer to this question is clearly 'no'. Nature has provided a refuse disposal service without which we would be quite helpless.

Another good reason for not killing all the pests is that we would in the process kill many animals which we regard as useful, and we would also be destroying the natural enemies of many other animals. These animals would then increase in numbers, quite unchecked, and some would in their turn come to be regarded as pests.

Insects, especially, have an important part to play in the great natural 'food chains'. Think how many animals live on insects, and in their turn provide food for animals, and finally for man.

But most important of all is the part insects play in the life of plants. Very many plants rely on insects for pollination, and the book in this series on *Flowers and their visitors* will tell you about this in more detail. Since plants supply some of our oxygen as a product of photosynthesis, the part played by such insects in ensuring that plant life continues is vital to animal life as well. The butterfly and the bumblebee may not seem very important, but without insects such as these there would be fewer plants, probably no animals, and almost certainly no mankind.

Recognising animals

Many people who see an animal they don't recognise, promptly kill it and then, perhaps, look more closely to see what it was. We kill millions of animals like this. Slow-worms are killed as though they were dangerous snakes, moths and flies of all kinds are swatted or sprayed at first sight, and even bees are sometimes mistaken for wasps.

Knowing about nature, recognising animals for what they are, and understanding the life histories of pests is the first step in the fight against them.

Opposite: Brown rats plundering eggs

Left: A dead brown rat
Below: A black rat

Brown rat *Rattus norvegicus*

This is one of the worst dangers to public health, and it has many popular names, such as sewer rat and grey rat. Its colour is greyish brown, with various shadings of both grey and brown. Adults can grow up to 40 or 50 cm long, including the tail. The length of the tail is about $\frac{3}{7}$ of the total length, and it is covered with scales. As is suggested by the name sewer rat, the brown rat swims well, and eats all kinds of filth.

Brown rats can transmit a number of diseases, including Weil's disease, foot and mouth disease, swine fever, paratyphoid and rat-bite fever.

Black rat *Rattus rattus*

This is much less common than the brown rat, and is smaller; it does not normally grow above 30–35 cm long and the tail is noticeably longer than the body. Its ears are bigger than those of brown rats, and the snout is pointed.

Black rats are mainly restricted to harbour towns, but since these rats do not swim special precautions are taken to see that they are kept aboard the ships which carry them. It was the black rats which brought the bubonic plague, or Black Death, to Europe in the Middle Ages.

Water rat or water vole
Arvicola amphibius

This rodent looks like a big field mouse, growing to a length of 15 cm including the tail. It rarely goes into a house, but burrows underground throwing up the soil, which may then resemble 'mole-hills'. It swims well. Because it is hard to kill with poisons it is usually caught in traps.

These animals can cause massive

Right: House mouse
Below: Water rat or water vole

damage to crops because they live on the roots of plants, eating anything they find as they burrow along underground. Because they lead such a hidden life, they are often not noticed until a gardener suddenly sees his plants, bushes and even trees dying without apparent cause.

Another animal which looks rather like a swimming rat is the coypu, *Myocastor coypus*. This is not native to Britain, but was imported from South America and some escapes occured. It is a large animal and can grow up to a metre long including the tail. It is fairly harmless, living mainly on rushes and reeds. In fact in some German towns it is used to keep canals free from waterplants.

House mouse   *Mus musculus*

The true house mouse is quite a large animal, with a body about 9 cm long, and a tail a further 9 cm. It is an even greyish-brown, and several varieties occur in this country.

House mice can run very fast and climb well. They eat almost anything, but prefer bread, grain, cheese, bacon, sugar and other foodstuffs, though they will make do with soap, shoe polish, and paper, all of which are made from vegetable or animal materials.

Mice build nests in the most surprising places, such as inside chairs or behind pictures. They produce a litter of 3–9 young every four or six weeks, so they can increase rapidly in numbers.

Other rodents which sometimes enter houses are the field mouse *Apodemus sylvaticus* and the harvest mouse, *Micromys minutus*.

Bedbug   *Cimex lectularius*

This human parasite is quite common. It lives by sucking warm human blood. It is 5–7 mm long, varying in colour from yellowish grey to blackish brown. It is a typical night animal, hiding in cracks by day, or behind wallpaper or pictures or in the joints or springs of beds. Then it emerges at night.

Only when the female is well fed will she lay her eggs, which she deposits in the cracks and crevices where she hides during the day. The eggs hatch in anything from one to three weeks, depending on the temperature of the room, and the nymphs look exactly like the adult animals, except that they are smaller. They can suck blood at once, and can start laying eggs in about seven weeks.

The bite of the bedbug is not very painful but causes an itch which lasts several days. They are less common than they once were.

Their presence in the house can sometimes be detected by a strange sweetish smell which they exude, but it is much more reliable to look for their droppings, which are black lumps the size of pin heads, and also for the empty skins shed by the nymphs.

Left: A bedbug much enlarged
Right: Clothes moth

Clothes moth
Tineola bissellicella

The moths we see fluttering about are mostly males in search of a female. The male usually dies after mating, and the female lays 50–100 eggs, which will hatch into caterpillars. These larvae feed on textiles, preferring wool or fur. Wool or fur alone does not make a very nourishing meal, so they usually look for a greasy stain or the greasy edge of a collar.

The true clothes moth (illustrated) is straw yellow in colour, with a wingspan of about 13 mm and no spots on its wings.

A second kind of moth sometimes found in the house is the fur moth, which is a little larger and has a few dark spots on its yellowish front wings. The larvae of this moth live in a kind of tube which they make out of threads. The larva has a black head, whereas the clothes moth larva is more brown in colour.

One can save oneself a great deal of misery by having clothes and furnishings mothproofed by a good firm. A cupboard from which moths are seen to emerge can be sprayed with an insecticide, but the instructions must be read carefully, because some insecticides stain clothes yellow.

BEETLES

a. *Black-tailed beetle*
b. *Woodworm beetle (see page 22)*
c. *Carpet beetle (see page 23)*
d. *Fur beetle (see page 23)*
e. *Cellar beetle (see page 23)*
f. *Shining niptus (see page 24)*
g. *Mealworm beetle (see page 24)*
h. *Bacon beetle (see page 25)*
i. *Spider beetle (see page 25)*
j. *Grain weevil (see page 25)*

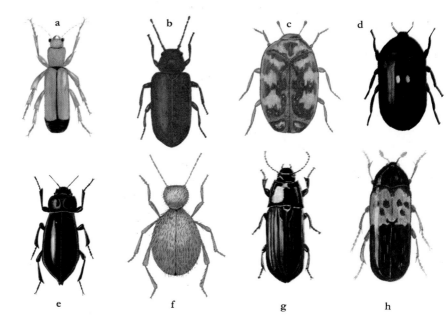

The floors and shelves of the cupboard can be washed with soap, so that the eggs and larvae in the cracks are killed.

There is no need to use aerosol sprays on adult moths. A fly swat is a better way of killing them.

Black-tailed beetle
Nacerdes melanura

This fairly large beetle can be 15 mm long. The larvae prefer to live in old wood, such as unused lengths of timber left under the floor-boards. They can overrun a house, especially in summer.

The best way of controlling them is to remove oddments of old wood, but if this is difficult one can spray a good insecticide under the floor. However, this may not get deep enough into the wood to kill the larvae. Adult beetles should be killed, but there is no need to spray insecticides at them.

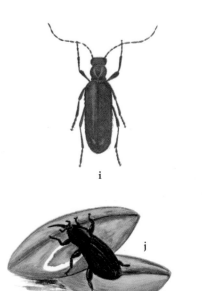

Above: Woodworm beetle   Below: Woodworm larva

Woodworm   *Anobium species*

'Woodworm' is the collective name for the larvae of several kinds of beetles which we can find in furniture, cupboards, floors and roof joists. The beetles are only a few millimetres in length, and they usually fly around at night, so they are not often seen. The presence of woodworm larvae is detected from the small round holes which they gnaw in the wood, and the powdery dust underneath the holes.

A fertilised female woodworm beetle looks for soft unpainted wood in which to lay her eggs, and often chooses the plywood back of a sideboard or the under-side of a chair seat. After a time the larvae emerge, and immediately start boring into the wood. Each larva can stay up to three years in the wood before the damage becomes obvious; after pupating, the adult beetle makes its way out and one can see the holes.

A well known species is the death-watch beetle, which causes a tapping noise by knocking its head against the wood—an eery sound best heard in the quiet of the night.

Carpet beetle
Anthrenus scrophulariae

Until about 1960 these beetles lived out of doors. Suddenly they moved inside and the larvae began to feed on woollens, carpets, furs and stuffed animals. The larvae are only a few millimetres long, white and brown striped, and rather hairy. Unlike clothes moth larvae, which shave wool bare, carpet beetle larvae make holes in the fabric. The beetles themselves are 2–4 mm long and beautifully coloured.

Sometimes the larvae of the carpet beetle develop in dead mice or rats.

Methods of control are the same as with the clothes moth.

Cellar beetles

Fur beetle *Attagenus pellio*

This beetle, 4–5 mm long, is rare in the house. It is completely black, except for a white patch on each wing shield. The larvae are slightly bigger and darker than those of the carpet beetle, and have a long plume at the tip of the tail.

Because fur is very expensive, these beetles can do costly damage, but they can be fairly easily controlled by spraying fur clothes with an insecticide as a precaution.

Cellar beetle *Blaps mucronata*

Found in cellars, under chests or boxes, or under floorboards, these animals grow up to 25 mm long. They can sometimes emerge through the cracks in the floorboards and invade a house. They can be fairly easily caught by laying down a wet floor cloth. Since they love damp they will usually crawl on to it, and can then be killed.

The larvae live in damp old wood and in rotting plants so they do not do much damage. Spraying with insecticide is pointless, because the beetles usually appear one at a time. Sometimes sprinkling an insecticide in a dry part of the cellar helps.

Mealworm beetle and larva

Shining niptus or golden spider beetle *Niptus holoceucus*

These are usually found in wash basins or bath tubs. They are 4–5 mm long and are often mistaken for bedbugs. The larvae live a hidden life, often in thatched roofs, or in old straw mattresses. They do little damage.

Occasionally these beetles may eat textiles, usually choosing silk or artificial silk. They have been known to eat nylon. Blocking their entrance holes (usually air ducts, cracks by radiators, etc) can be a good way of keeping them out of living areas. There is little point in using insecticides, because the beetles never appear in great numbers.

Mealworm beetle or 'hardback' *Tenebrio molitor*

Mealworms can be bought as petfood for birds and reptiles. They are the larvae of black beetles about 2 cm long, which are quite often found in houses. They eat stocks of cereals, but do little other damage. It is not even necessary to throw away the affected food—careful sifting and destruction of mealworms is enough.

If the cereal stocks are left for too long, the mealworms pupate and then the house (or more often shop or warehouse) can be filled with the adult beetles, which are often mistaken for cockroaches. They do no harm, and the best method of getting rid of them is to put a jar of flour or oats somewhere. The beetles will make for it in order to deposit their eggs. Then they can be killed.

Bacon beetle
Dermestes lardarius

There are a number of varieties of bacon beetle in this country, but the commonest is a black beetle about 8 mm long, with a diagonal grey band on each wing shield. Both the adults and the larvae feed mainly on bacon, ham, smoked meats, sausage and dried fish, but they also feed on fur and leather. The larvae can do extensive damage.

The affected goods must be thoroughly cleared of the larvae; food must then be salted, while furs can be treated with insecticide. Adult beetles can be caught by putting out a strongly smelling piece of old cheese.

The larvae are fairly big and have a lot of hair. They are whitish yellow with brown crossbands.

Spider beetle *Ptinus fur*

These rarely grow longer than 2 mm but they can damage dry foodstuffs, such as herbs and vegetables. 'Storage insects' like these, which damage food stocks, cannot be fought with insecticides, which would damage the food. The food has to be thrown away. The only remedy is to prevent them getting in by storing food in properly sealed containers.

Grain weevil
Calandra granaria

These are typical 'storage insects', often found in warehouses. They have a trunk-like snout at the head and are about 4 mm long. As the name suggests, they eat all sorts of grain, and also pasta (spaghetti, etc).

The females lay their eggs each in a separate grain, and the larva eats away the contents of the grain. The best treatment is to throw the food away, but it can be treated with a dry heat of at least 60° for five minutes to destroy the larvae.

Occasionally these beetles spread out from a pantry over a whole house. Spraying cracks with insecticide can give good results, but the important thing is that the beetles should find nothing edible.

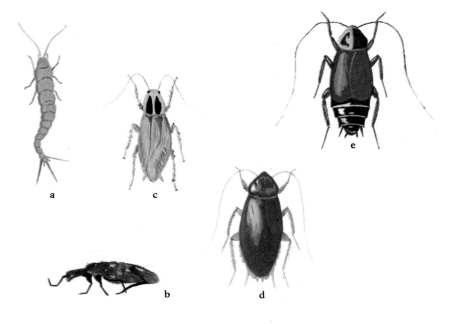

a. *Silverfish*
b. *Spring-tail*
c. *German cockroach*
d. *American cockroach*
e. *Common cockroach*

Silverfish *Lepisma saccharina*

These swift silver-coloured animals, less than 1 cm long, are active at night, usually in cupboards under the sink or in the cellars of damp houses. They eat mainly flour, sugar and starch. They can cause damage in houses by eating the paste behind wallpaper or the glue of book bindings.

Spraying insecticide where they are seen regularly may help, but their scaly outsides make powder insecticides useless unless they eat it. They can be caught using bait such as a piece of banana peel, a raw potato or some boiled starch.

The silverfish has a relative, the fire-brat, *Thermobia domestica,* which grows a little larger and is brown in colour. It occurs in dry warm places, especially in temperatures above 35°C. Way of life and methods of control are similar to those of the silverfish.

Spring-tail
Lepidocyrtinus divinatorius

These can occur in large numbers on damp mossy roofs, in damp plant boxes and trays. They move forward by hopping, and are often mistaken for fleas. They can get into houses, and become almost a plague. Though they are harmless to man, they sometimes eat raw potatoes.

They can be destroyed by insecticides, or by replacing the old earth in a plant tray by new. On roofs they can be removed by dissolving 10 grammes of copper sulphate in 1000 litres of water, and spraying this on the roof.

Their hopping is done by means of a 'tail' which is bent underneath their body and with which they push themselves off.

German cockroach
Blattella germanica

Of the three main types of cockroach found in Britain, this is the smallest. It is light brown, and about 14 mm long. Both male and females can fly well, but they

*Right: Female common
cockroach
Below: American cockroaches*

rarely use their wings. Cockroaches do not like the light, and hide in cracks and holes during the day. In houses they are usually found in kitchens and bathrooms.

The females have an egg 'purse' on their abdomens in which there are about forty eggs. The riper the eggs, the more the egg purse protrudes. The cockroach carries the egg purse until just before the young hatch.

Common cockroach
Blatta orientalis

The common cockroach is dark brown to blue-black and can be up to 28 mm long. Only the male of this kind is winged, and he rarely flies. The egg purse containing 15–16 eggs, is deposited by the female in a hidden spot, and can stay there for two or three months before the young hatch. These animals originally came from Asia and were imported along with merchandise.

American cockroach
Periplaneta americana

The biggest cockroach in this country, it can grow up to 45 mm long. Both males and females have wings. The egg purse can be left for a long time before the eggs hatch. This cockroach is not common, except on ships.

The best defence against cockroaches is to leave no food for them. They are not easily destroyed except by fumigation, though several dustings of insecticides may have a gradual effect. Pest control officers usually have more powerful insecticides for use against cockroaches.

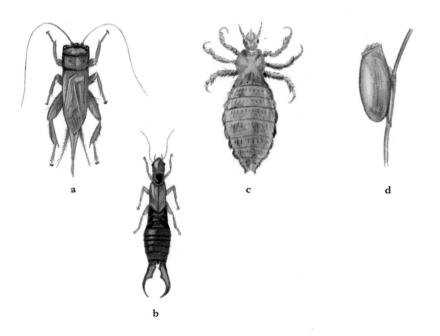

a. *House cricket*
b. *Common earwig*
c. *Head louse*
d. *The egg of a head louse—
   a nit*

House cricket
Actheta domesticus

In the past it used to be quite common to hear the irritating chirping of these grasshopper-like animals in the house; then they seemed to disappear, but now they seem to be coming back, especially in centrally heated flats. They are light brown, and about 2 cm long. They do not do much harm, eating mainly vegetable matter and occasionally paper. It is their chirping which is irritating.

They can jump about 25 cm, but they usually crawl instead, and they only appear at dusk and in the night. It is hard to find their lairs to use insecticide, so they have to be caught one by one.

Common earwig
Forficula auricularia

Earwigs can be found in most gardens, and often find their way into the house. They prefer to live in cracks in doors and windows. They are dark brown animals, 10–15 mm long. No-one knows how they got the name earwig, because they certainly are not found in human ears! At the lower end of their body they have a vicious looking pair of pincers, which they use to fold their wings and also as a weapon in fights among themselves. They can pinch your finger with these, but it is not usually painful.

Sprinkling powder along the wall usually keeps earwigs outside the house, and a good method of catching them is to attract them to an inverted flowerpot full of damp hay or wood shavings.

Head louse
Pediculus humanus capitis

Long hair does not encourage head lice, but unwashed hair may. Lice are pale yellow or greyish animals about 2 mm long, which live in the hair of the head, or occasionally in eyebrows or beards. Their legs have claws by means of which they hold on to the hairs. They feed several times a day on human blood. The eggs (nits) are laid on short hairs behind the ears or on the neck. The young lice hatch after about six days and at once begin feeding on blood. They are adult within eighteen days. Lice only live for about eight weeks, but each female may lay fifty to a hundred eggs. It is not known whether they carry disease.

It used to be necessary to shave the head, and use special soaps, but these soaps are useless against modern lice. Nowadays special shampoos and lotions are successfully used against nits and lice.

Body louse
Pediculus humanus corporis

Without a microscope, it is almost impossible to tell this creature from a head louse, though it is slightly larger and sometimes a little darker. It never lives on the hair but always on the body. The eggs are stuck to clothes, especially to collars and cuffs and to underwear.

Body lice can transmit typhus. Contaminated clothing should be boiled thoroughly and the body

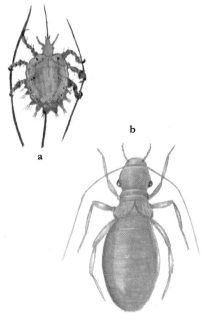

a. *Crab louse*
b. *Booklouse*

should be thoroughly washed with soap. Outer clothing should also be de-loused in a special hot-air oven, as also should infested bedding.

Crab louse *Phthirus pubis*

Crab lice are smaller than head or clothes lice and live mainly in the pubic hair or in the armpits. They grow to about 1·5 mm and like other lice they live on human blood. Contamination usually occurs through direct contact with other people who have crab lice.

The crab louse has a lifespan of about three weeks, during which the female produces about 25 eggs which stick to the hair. If the louse is removed from a human body, it will die within ten hours.

To get rid of them one must shave the affected area completely and carefully wash the skin with soap. In cases of severe infestation, a doctor can prescribe a special ointment.

Booklouse
Liposcelis divinatorius

These are not true lice, but belong to a different group of insects. Colonies can multiply rapidly in damp houses. They do little real damage, living on the paste behind wallpaper or in books, though they may sometimes eat paper. They move along rather fast, but stop frequently.

They can become a nuisance in the stuffing of mattresses or in upholstery, and the furniture then has to be treated in a hot air oven.

They will not choose to live in a well-lit, well-ventilated house. A light spraying of insecticide can help to destroy them.

a. *Human flea*
b. *The head of a human flea*
c. *The head of a dog flea*
d. *The head of a cat flea*
  (enlarged)
e. *A dog flea*

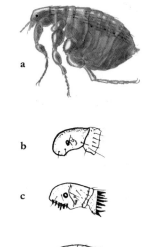

Human flea *Pulex irritans*

The human flea is found all over the world. In the warm summer months they can become a plague. Usually they live no longer than three or four months, though under certain circumstances they can live longer.

The females can lay as many as 450 eggs in cracks under skirting boards or between floorboards, because, unlike the adults, the larvae do not eat blood, but live on all sorts of rubbish including the droppings of adult fleas.

The eggs hatch after 4–12 days, and about a week after hatching, the larvae pupate. The larval stage can last up to 80 days if conditions are unfavourable. The pupa stage lasts about six days, but it has been known to take 239 days!

Fleas find their hosts in three ways:

a. By heat radiated from the host, which the flea can sense.
b. By smell. Every animal, including man, has its own smell, which is attractive to its own sort of flea (and there are 1300 known species of flea).
c. By air currents. Fleas always walk into the draught, which helps them find their hosts more quickly.

Other fleas which can become a nuisance are the dog flea and the cat flea. These will attack humans if no dog or cat is available.

Fleas can be destroyed quite easily by spraying insecticide fairly vigorously into floor cracks and under skirting boards, but these insecticides should never be allowed to touch the skin. Special powders can be bought for treating pets which are infested with fleas.

Common gnat *Culex pipiens*

At most 6 mm long, this can nevertheless be quite a nuisance to man. It pierces the skin with its long proboscis and gorges itself on blood.

The wings of this species have no spots and are slightly irridescent. They are most active in the summer and early autumn. The larvae live in water. There can be several generations a year, and only the females of the last generation survive the winter, in cellars, stables and attics.

The ringed mosquito, *Theobaldia annulata,* with its white ringed abdomen and legs, is a little bigger, growing to 9 mm. It also has spotted wings, and is found even in the late autumn, and sometimes in houses during the winter.

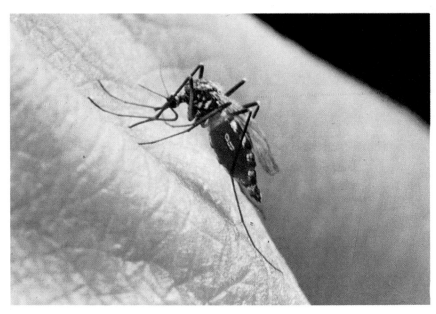

Malaria mosquitoes need water for their life cycle because the larvae and pupae live in water. In countries where malaria is a serious problem, open water is sometimes seriously polluted by chemicals in an attempt to stamp out the mosquitoes. Mosquitoes can also use pools of water which may form under floors, and here it is easier to use insecticides.

Malaria mosquitoes can be distinguished from gnats and other mosquitoes by their resting position, in which the abdomen and hind legs slant upwards, as you can see in diagrams (c) and (d).

Above: A common gnat sucking blood

Below:
a. Common gnat
b. Malaria mosquito
c. Gnat in resting position
d. Mosquito in resting position

Only the females of these gnats suck blood, the males feed on plant juices. They can be controlled by screens in windows and by spraying with insecticide.

Malaria mosquito
Anopheles maculipennis

This mosquito is much more dangerous than the common gnat, because it transmits malaria. But it can only do so when it has sucked blood from a malaria patient.

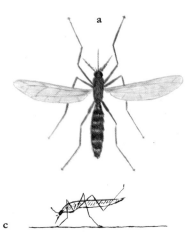

House fly

House fly *Musca domestica*

This is the kind of fly we usually mean when we talk vaguely about 'flies'. There is another very similar but slightly smaller kind, the lesser house fly, *Fannia cannicularis*, which is found in cities. They live wherever we live.

The house fly is about 8 mm long, with large chocolate coloured eyes. Its chest is greyish and the abdomen brownish; the wings are transparent. The flies rarely live longer than 3–4 months but those which find a lot of sugar can live longer. There can be as many as thirteen generations born in one year.

Flies can be best kept out of the house by means of screens, and, once inside, a good airing will usually drive them away since they hate draughts.

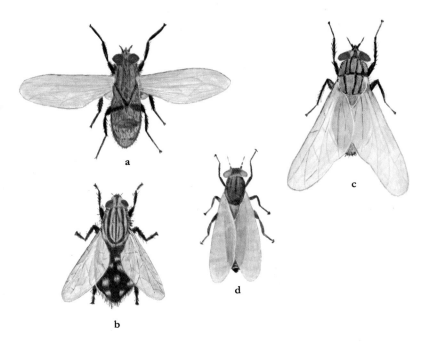

a. *House fly*
b. *Grey fleshfly*
c. *Stable fly*
d. *Horsefly*

Fleshfly   *Sarcophaga carnaria*
These are grey with red eyes and an abdomen chequered like a chess board, and are about 15 mm long. They lay their eggs in rotting meat and the eggs hatch immediately after laying. The larvae live on the rotting meat. Fleshflies rarely come into the house unless there is a dead mouse or rat under the floor or a dead bird in a vent or chimney. Then there is a chance that the flies will look for an escape route through the house. They can easily be chased out of a window, or if not they can be trapped by putting a piece of meat in a bottle with a very narrow neck.

Stable fly   *Stomoxys calcitrans*
It is hard at first sight to tell this from the house fly, but on closer inspection you will see the horn-like proboscis which can give a painful bite—especially when a storm is brewing. This fly is more common in the country than in towns as it lays its eggs chiefly in cow and horse dung.

Forest flies   *Hippoboscidae*
These are not illustrated, but see the book on *Insects* in this series.

They are bloodsuckers living as parasites on mammals and birds, and some of them are so used to this way of life that they no longer have wings. On rare occasions a forest fly may enter a house, and it can bite painfully. However, they can easily be caught.

Horseflies   *Tabanus species*
Only the females suck blood, but they do it so fiercely that blood may flow from the wound after the bite. They fly quietly and often land on unprotected parts of the body, though their proboscis is strong enough to pierce through clothing.

Top: Blue fleshfly
Below: Stable fly

They are common near ponds, lakes and marshy ground, and sometimes come into gardens, especially where there is a ditch near by, but rarely enter a house. The commonest is the horse fly, *Tabanus bovinus* which grows to a size of nearly 2·5 cm. Much smaller is the related cleg *Chrysozoma pluvialis,* which is about 10 mm long.

The effect of a horsefly's attack depends on the victim. Some people find it very painful but there are no after effects, whilst other people are left with a large white itching spot.

Honeybee   *Apis mellifica*

Although these are useful, we prefer them in the garden and not in the house. They sometimes fly in during the summer,

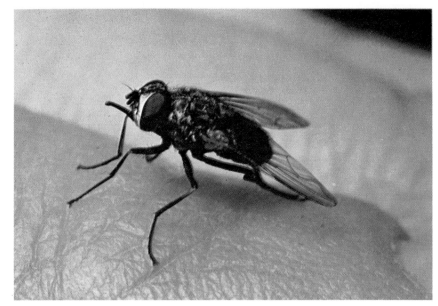

Left: Honeybees

Below:
a. Honeybee
b. Common wasp
Photograph of a common wasp

a　　　　　　　　b

and will usually fly out again of their own accord. Even if they land on you, they will usually fly away again if you do not panic. Bees only sting when frightened. A bee sting can be painful, because the sting breaks off and is left in the wound.

Common wasp *Vespa vulgaris*

Wasps deliberately come into the house in summer in search of sweet foods. If a stray wasp comes in it will usually fly away again when it has finished eating. It is rather different if you have a nest in or near the house, and it should be destroyed.

In winter the whole colony dies out, except the queen, so if you destroy any wasps you see in early spring that will probably be one nest less in summer. Wasps can sting several times in succession and their stings are painful. A large number of wasp stings at one time can be dangerous.

Don't chase a wasp as soon as it enters the house. Wait for it to settle down, then try to catch it with a tumbler and a piece of cardboard.

As well as the common wasp, we sometimes find hornets in the house.

Garden black ant *Lasius niger*

These small greedy creatures can bring people to despair when they invade a house in their thousands. The ants we find in the house are the 'workers' whose task is to feed the larvae and the queen. They have no wings.

In late summer the males and the new queens are born, and these do have wings. They swarm to mate and then the males die and the queens look for suitable places to start new nests.

Ants don't do much damage in the house, but they can be a nuisance if their nest is not destroyed in time. They never attack, but they can defend themselves with their sharp jaws, and at the same time squirt acid into the wound, giving a burning sensation.

Pharaoh's ant
Monomorium pharaonis

This small, yellow-brown ant came originally from tropical countries, but it is rapidly spreading in Europe and in Britain, so we may see many more of them in the future. They like warmth, and can be a plague in bakeries, kitchens, restaurants and hospitals.

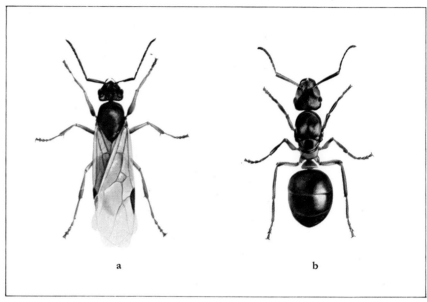

a. Garden black ant, queen   b. Garden black ant, male

The queens are a little bigger than the workers, and there may be a large number in each nest, so there is a strong chance of one getting into a house. Within a few months there is a colony of ants.

Regular cleaning out in the larder can prevent trouble, as well as storing paper-packaged goods in sealed containers. Attempts to block up the entrances to the nest are usually unsuccessful because the ants can get through the smallest gap.

Cellar slug *Limax flavius*

Slugs leave trails of silvery dried up slime, which is secreted from their crawling foot. If these trails are found inside the house, it is usually the cellar slug which has made them. It has no shell and hides in damp dark places during the day, coming out at night in search of vegetable food. It is a brownish animal about 10 cm long, which can shrink to about half its normal length when touched.

Cellar slugs are bisexual (male

a. Garden black ant, worker
b. Pharaoh's ant
c. Cellar slug
d. Woodlouse
Photograph of a woodlouse

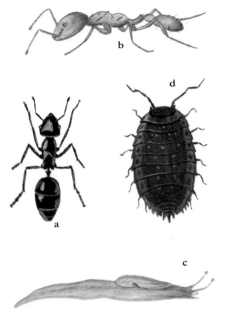

and female at the same time) which means that any two slugs can fertilise one another. They lay 200–300 eggs among rotting vegetable matter and the young slugs emerge after a few weeks.

People sometimes recommend killing slugs with salt, but this kills them slowly and messily. It is better to use a slug-killer, and these are available under several brand names. One can also trap them by pouring some beer into a saucer. They are attracted by the beer and then they can be killed in boiling water. Apart from their slimy trails, they do little damage in the house.

Other kinds of slug get into houses by accident, but really belong in the garden, where their relatives the snails are also found, damaging plants. Most poisons you might use to kill them will probably do more harm to the plants than the snails do, so it is better to kill the snails and slugs one by one.

Woodlouse *Oniscus species*

This animal is not an insect but a crustacean. There are several species all of which live on vegetable matter. In daytime they hide under stones, in rubbish, in boxes, etc, and they do not do a great deal of damage.

As with earwigs, they can be caught in an upturned flowerpot filled with damp hay, which will attract the animals as a hiding place.

Left: Brown centipede with a dead earthworm
Below: Drawing of a brown centipede

Brown centipede
Lithobius forficatus

The name centipede ('hundred legs') is an exaggeration, because these animals rarely have more than fifteen pairs of legs. They hunt all kinds of insects and spiders, killing them with their powerful jaws. These are hollow, and contain a poison gland.

Centipedes are not in the least harmful; indeed they help us by destroying other vermin, and so long as they don't harm us there is no point in interfering with them. If one should stray into a house, it can easily be caught and released outside. They can bite with their jaws, but the bite scarcely hurts at all. Often they cannot pierce our skin.

Scabies mite   *Sarcoptes scabei*

This tiny arachnid (spider) causes the itching illness scabies. The female burrows v-shaped passages just under the skin, causing a terrible itch, usually in a place where the skin is thin, for instance between the fingers or on the inside of the wrists. Then the female lays about 50 eggs in the passage she has made and the young emerge about a week later. The males walk up and down over the skin during the night, which also causes itching. The mites can scarcely be seen with the naked eye.

Redfowl mite
Dermanyssus gallinae

These occur in the nests of all kinds of birds, living especially on the blood of the chicks. When the young birds leave the nest, the mites have to find a new source of food, so they sometimes come into houses in search of new hosts—us. These mites can multiply so fast that the walls of a bedroom may be black with them. Because they cannot suck

a. Scabies mite
b. Redfowl mite
c. House spider
d. Dog tick
The photograph on the far right
shows a garden spider in its web

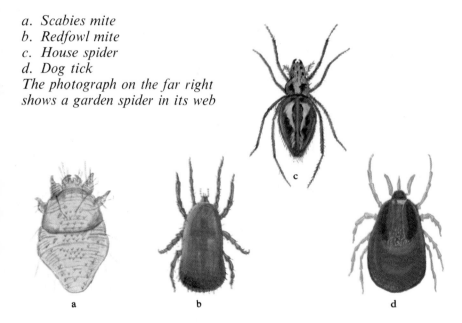

a   b   c   d

easily through a thick skin, they usually choose young children as their victims, causing a severe rash.

There is no way of keeping the mites out because they are so small, and the best way of getting rid of them is by using an insecticide. Similar mites can infest chickens, pigeons and cage birds, which can be treated with pesticides available from pet shops.

House spider
Tegeneria domestica

It is hard to understand why some people have such a deep fear of spiders. Although some kinds can bite if we pick them up, there is not one British spider which is harmful. They keep down other pests and they rarely become a plague themselves.

The house spider makes a funnel-shaped web in a corner or near a window, and catches all kinds of insects. If you don't like the spider's web in the room, then you can catch the spider and let it go elsewhere, but there is no good reason to kill a spider.

Dog tick   *Sarcoptes canis*

The females of these animals live on blood, boring into the dog's skin to suck blood. They hold on with the claws on their legs and it is very hard to pull them out. Often the head breaks off before the tick will let go, and the head will be left in the dog's skin, causing an inflammation. Human beings can also be attacked by ticks.

Before they start sucking, they are about 1·5 mm long, but when they have gorged themselves with blood they are round and nearly 10 mm long. The best treatment is to let a drop of vinegar or iodine fall on to the ticks, which makes them let go.

The fight against pests

Prevention

Prevention is better than cure. It is not too difficult to keep pests out of the house, if you know how to set about it. The first thing to realise is that pests do not only plague other people: they can be a nuisance to *you*. Insects, rats and mice breed fast and are always looking for new places to colonise. They could choose *your* house, however clean you may be.

THE FIGHT AGAINST RATS AND MICE

In order to keep out rats and mice we should make sure that there are no holes in the walls (particularly where pipes enter), that doors and windows shut properly, that air vents are not wide enough to let mice through, and that the foundations are too deep for rats to dig under.

The main thing, though, is to make sure that they cannot find food. Dustbins should always be kept closed, and if they are kept under cover they should be put out on the morning the dustmen call and not the night before.

If you feed the birds in the park, don't do it in the late afternoon and evening. Most people mean to be kind when they feed the ducks, but actually the birds get too fat on this kind of food, and also too lazy to find food for themselves. If you like feeding birds, the best time to do it is in winter, during snow or frost. At such a time the birds really do have difficulty finding food. If you feed towards evening, some of the food may not be eaten by birds, but by the twilight creatures, especially rats.

Rats can dig beneath shallow foundations. As a result the wall sinks and a crack forms. This can be very expensive to repair.

Natural enemies

A hedgehog or a weasel in the garden is the best and cheapest rat catcher you can get, though you have to keep chickens and pigeons away from them or you might prefer to have the rats rather than the weasel.

A good dog—especially one of the small breeds —can be a good rat catcher, but do not rely on cats. Most cats will run away from a large rat, and there are even cases of rats killing cats. Cats will certainly help by catching mice, provided they are not given too much food. Cats on farms are sometimes kept half-starved to make them good mousers, but that would be rather hard on a pet cat.

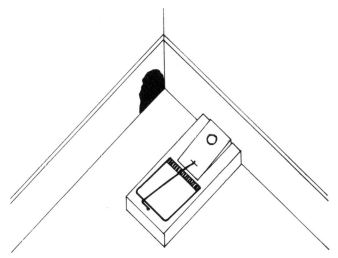

The right way to set a trap

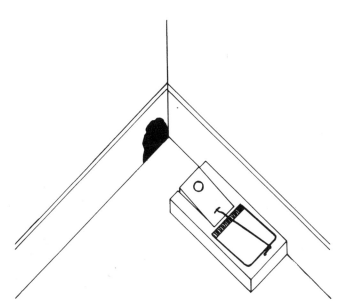

The wrong way to set a trap

Traps

There are several kinds of trap available, but the old-fashioned snap-trap is probably still the best. This kind has the advantage that it kills the animal immediately so you are not left with a live rat or mouse to dispose of.

Setting a mouse trap is not as easy as most people think. Firstly, the placing is important. Rats and mice have a fear of open spaces. They usually move along the edges of a room, and rarely cross directly from one side to the other. Outdoors, too, they walk beside walls or along the edge of water, so that they need watch only one way for an attacker. So putting a trap in the middle of a room is rather pointless.

Because the animals will walk round a small obstacle more easily than round a large one, it is best to place the trap with the short side against the wall so that it sticks out into the room. The bait should be nearest to the wall.

One must take care that there is no human smell on the trap. If so, the animals will simply not touch the bait. You can get round this by wearing gloves.

It is important that the trap should be lightly sprung, ready to snap at the slightest touch, otherwise you may find the bait gone but no mouse in the trap. Be careful of your own fingers, because the spring is quite powerful.

Rat poisons

Many poisons have been tried on rats and mice, often with good results. But unfortunately these poisons have also been fatal to man and domestic pets. Several famous Victorian murders were carried out with rat poisons such as arsenic which could at that time be bought freely in the shops.

These poisons cause the animal a very painful death, and if we intend to kill them we should try to do it in a painless way. Besides, rats are intelligent and if one of their number dies in agony after eating what looked like an appetising meal, the rest of the group will never touch it and a new bait must be tried.

At one time a kind of biscuit containing an extract from a special Mediterranean onion was used. Only a small quantity would kill a rat, but it tasted terribly bitter. The rat 'biscuits' disappeared quite fast, so people assumed they were a success, but research showed that the rats were only taking the biscuits either as food store for the winter or even as bedding for the nest.

Nowadays there are rat poisons called warfarin and coumarin, which are far less dangerous to man and domestic pets. Warfarin is sold as a powder, to be mixed with a bait, usually bread or wheat. The great advantage is that the animal dies without its fellows knowing why, because death is not immediate.

Warfarin causes certain changes in the blood and in the blood vessels. After the animal has been eating the poison for some days, internal bleeding starts and the animal dies from weakness. The effect is similar to a man being bled to death by leeches, which is a painless death. We think that rats and mice die painlessly from warfarin—though of course we have no way of being sure.

One problem with warfarin is that the internal bleeding makes the rat feel cold, and he will look for a warm place to die. This is usually the nest, but it can be a warm part of the house, such as under the floor near the stove, in which case there may be a bad smell as a result.

CONTROLLING INSECTS AND LICE

In theory insects are best controlled in the same way as mice, by prevention rather than cure. We can keep flying insects out of the house by putting mesh screens over doors and windows, and crawling insects can be kept out by blocking cracks and crannies. It is worth checking newly bought food, especially fruit, to see that no food-eating pests are brought into the house.

Good bodily and domestic hygiene is the best way of preventing parasites such as fleas and lice from gaining a hold.

Natural enemies

In agriculture pests are quite often controlled nowadays by introducing their natural enemies. For example, ichneumon flies (parasitic wasps) are used to control some kinds of beetle. But of course we cannot use this method in the home, at least not on any large scale. Releasing shrews to catch cockroaches or bats to catch flying insects would have obvious disadvantages!

Even so, we can use the method on a small scale. There is no harm in leaving a cobweb over the cellar window, as the spiders will keep the gnat and fly population under control. If you are lucky enough to have toads nearby, they help in the fight against slugs and crawling insects, and ladybirds will keep aphids in check in the garden.

Traps

Insect traps are occasionally sold in shops, but they rarely have much effect.

Home-made traps are sometimes useful. For example wasps can be enticed away from the house by putting out a jam jar containing some sugary liquid, perhaps with a paper lid through which you have pushed a knitting needle— making a hole large enough for the wasps to enter but impossible to get out of.

Cockroaches can sometimes be caught by means of a jam jar filled with coffee dregs up to about 3–4 cm. The inside of the jam jar has to be clean, or the cockroaches will be able to climb out.

Earwigs and woodlice are sometimes caught with an upside-down flowerpot, half filled with moist hay or wood shavings, in which the animals may shelter. They can then be killed or moved elsewhere.

The spider is one natural enemy we can use to keep down flying insects

Poison

Poison is the simplest way of fighting insects and similar pests, though it is not always the best way. Insecticides can be divided as follows:

a. bait with poison added
b. insect powders
c. aerosol sprays
d. strips

Bait

There are many old household recipes by which different insects can be killed. Usually they are made by adding poison to a substance the animal likes to eat. Usually these poisons are 'irritants'—that is, they are taken in at the mouth and begin to work only when they reach the stomach.

Insect powders

These are powders which must be sprinkled where the pests are usually seen. The animals walk through the powder.

If we walked through a poisonous powder knee-high, we would be unharmed unless the fumes were poisonous. Why should an insect's legs be more vulnerable? An insect's anatomy is very different from ours. Its nervous system is a complex system of nerve knots and nerve fibres. Some of the nerve fibres are to be found on the legs. When an insect walks through the poisonous powder its nervous system is directly affected, the nerve knots are destroyed and the animal dies. This is called a 'contact poison'.

Aerosol sprays

Aerosols work by pushing out a liquid poison under pressure, and the label usually tells us that it will kill any vermin we may want to kill.

If the poison kills so many different animals, we may well ask ourselves what it does not kill. There is usually a warning on the label not to stay in the room you have sprayed, but many people do not read the label. They happily spray around them like a small boy with a toy machine-gun, forgetting that people, animals they do not want to harm, and plants will all be affected by the poison. And the end result may be to kill four or five flies! There is nothing wrong with aerosol sprays, but they must be used carefully.

The effect of aerosol insecticides is based on spraying a cloud of poison around the insect, so that it has to 'breathe' it in. Some of the aerosols you can now buy act in this way but have a further effect. Any object which is sprayed retains a thin film of poison on it, and this acts as a contact poison, as well.

Strips

The old-fashioned fly-paper, which flies stuck to when they landed on it, was one kind of strip. The cluster of dead flies hanging from the lamp shade in summer used to be a common and rather unpleasant sight.

But the fly-paper did less harm than some modern strips, which release insecticide as a vapour. Always read and follow the instructions carefully before using one of these.

is minute, it can take a long time to obtain usable quantities. An air current was passed over 10 000 cockroaches for nine months in order to obtain eight grammes of the scent. Scientists are now able to make the scent by chemical means, but each insect species has its own scent, and it will take many years to make all of them.

Once the animals have been attracted, they have to be destroyed, and this is normally done by putting the source of the scent inside a trap from which there is no escape.

Selling fly-papers in 1870—with a specimen wrapped round his hat

New ways of controlling insects

Many insect species have a special scent by which the females can attract the males at mating time. This is particularly common when the males have wings but the females do not. The scent attracts males from several kilometres around.

In recent years scientists have used these scents for pest control. As the amount of scent

Sterilisation

Almost all insects, except a few aphids, reproduce by mating between male and female. If there are enough infertile males in one area, the mating is likely to be unsuccessful, and this has been tried as a method of pest control.

Male flies were sterilised by radiation in a laboratory and the resulting fertilised eggs did not develop. A large scale experiment was carried out on the island of Curaçao, north of Venezuela, where cattle suffered from the parasitic larva of a fly. Two months after the mating season, when the sterilised flies were released, it was clear that the eggs were infertile and that the fly had been more or less wiped out on Curaçao.

Following this success a 'fly-factory' was built in the USA where over five million flies a week were bred especially to be sterilised and released over areas where the fly is a pest.

Resistance

Some species gradually acquire immunity to poisons. This happens in much the same way as we acquire immunity to certain diseases, and as certain viruses acquire immunity to antibiotics. You can read more about this in the book on *Conservation* in this series.

Dangers

Obviously it is not good for us to take in some of the poisons we use against pests. The pesticides often find their way into water, and even into the air we breathe, so we cannot avoid taking them in in small quantities.

There are some harmful substances which we can take in in small quantities without doing any harm, because they are excreted by the body. But many other chemicals, such as DDT and mercury, are not excreted. They build up gradually in the body tissue. Many pesticides contain such chemicals.

Here is an example of how this happens: a pesticide seeps into a pond in drainage water. There it is absorbed by plankton, which do not absorb enough to die of it. The plankton are eaten by small crustaceans, which in their turn are eaten by small fish. Smaller fish are eaten by larger fish, and large fish are eaten by birds of prey. The amount of poison in one large fish may not be enough to kill it, but if a bird of prey eats ten such fish, the amount of poison may be enough to kill it or render its eggs infertile. Large fish are also eaten by humans.

Pesticides may soon destroy many animal species in this roundabout way, and some of the poisons have even been found in human breast milk.

Precautions

Fortunately governments are aware of these dangers, and to some extent they control the making and use of pesticides. But there are precautions we should all take when we use a pesticide.

a. Never use a spray anywhere near foodstuffs.
b. Keep tins of pesticide right away from small children.
c. Never spray a room if anyone is going to be using it.
d. Make sure you never breathe in any of the vapour as you spray.
e. Never sprinkle powder on clothing or in beds.
f. Never use the pesticide for any other purpose than the one stated on the container.
g. Try to discover the hideouts of the pest, and do not use the poison at random.
h. Start by making a plan of campaign, and then stick to it.

Details about some common pests

Rats

See the illustrations on pages 17–19. It is often said that there are as many rats as people. There are several different species of rat in this country—the black and brown rats, the musk-rat, the coypu and the water rat or water vole.

Musk-rats and coypus were originally brought here for their fur, but some escaped and a few colonies started. The coypu is fairly harmless, but the musk-rat can damage river and canal banks by undermining them.

As far as we can discover, the black rat came from central or south-east Asia, and was brought back to Europe in the ships of the Crusaders. In its natural state the black rat had lived in trees, but in Europe it immediately started to live in attics and in thatched roofs.

The brown rat comes from Mongolia, and until 1727 it rarely came further west than Russia. In that year there was a violent earthquake, and millions of rats crossed the Volga river and spread all over Europe. At the same time the black rat, which had been in Europe for several centuries, began to decrease in numbers.

People used to think that the brown rats, which are bigger and stronger, had driven the black ones out, but the animals have such different ways of life that they can rarely have met each other. In Poland and Russia today both species can be found living peacefully on the same farm, so the earlier theory has had to be abandoned.

Migration of the brown rat

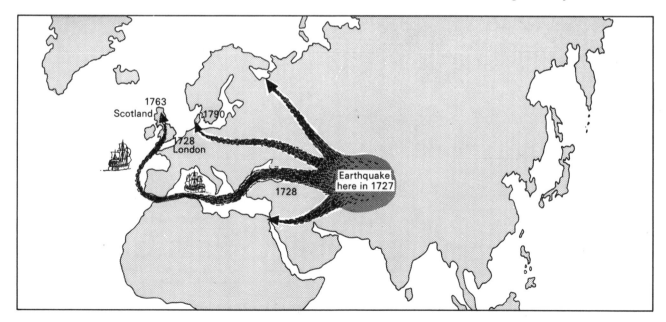

The brown rat naturally lives in a hole under the ground. In houses it generally chooses to live in cellars or in rooms at ground floor level. It so happened that, at the time the brown rat reached Europe, more stone houses were being built, and fewer thatched houses. Stone houses usually have cold attics and bedrooms, whereas thatch retains the heat in the top of the house. The black rat was originally from the tropics, and the new cold attics were unattractive to it, so gradually the black rats retreated.

The black rat was also attacked by man, as he discovered that it caused disease. Nowadays central heating in blocks of flats is making life easier again for the black rat, and they are occasionally seen in the big cities, especially ports.

Rats breed with amazing speed. The females can have litters between two and seven times a year, normally between eight and ten to a litter. They normally live for about eighteen months.

They are cannibalistic and kill any animal in the group which differs in colour or shape. One strange exception is that occasionally a 'rat-king' is found. This is a group of rats whose tails have grown together. Such a group cannot move about easily and has to be fed by other rats.

Brown rats can live anywhere where man can live. They are as much at home on the equator as in Eskimo huts. In Amsterdam a colony was found recently in a cold-storage warehouse, where the young were not naked at birth as they usually are but already had a covering of fur to protect them against the cold.

Bugs

See page 20. Bugs have strong mouths for biting and sucking. The jaws form a kind of beak or proboscis which is used for sucking blood or plant juices, depending on the species.

Apart from plant bugs which sometimes stray into the house and are quite harmless, there are two kinds of bugs which can trouble us—the bedbug and the flybug, *Reduvius personatus*.

Most insects have a metamorphosis as follows: egg—larva—pupa—adult. The larva is usually different in appearance from the adult. With the bugs this is not so. The larva looks almost exactly like the adult insect, and does not pupate: in this case, the young creature is usually called a nymph.

Although it is possible for one household to be contaminated by another, bedbugs are usually confined to one place. Even moving the bed from one end of a room to the other can sometimes stop the trouble for a while.

On the other hand they can easily be transported on clothes and luggage. Buying a second-hand bed could bring a plague of bedbugs. It is not known whether bedbugs can transmit diseases, but we do know that tuberculosis bacteria can survive for three or four days in the body of a bedbug.

The flybug rarely bites humans, and lives on smaller insects including bedbugs. One might call it a useful animal, but when it does bite it can be painful and research has shown that diseases can sometimes be transmitted by the bite. Flybugs are about 15 mm long.

Cockroaches

See pages 26–27. A plague of cockroaches is a very nasty experience. It can take a long time to get rid of them, and there is something repulsive about their hidden nocturnal life.

When you suddenly switch on a light in a kitchen where cockroaches live, you can see them scuttling for cover across the floor. They can make themselves almost flat in order to crawl through the narrowest opening. Cockroaches have an incomplete metamorphosis. The eggs are kept in a little 'purse' on the abdomen of the female. Some species keep this purse until just before the young hatch, others place it in a hidden spot after a few days.

Cockroaches will eat anything. If they can find nothing better, they will eat paper, softboard, clothing, their dead fellows and other insects.

A plague of cockroaches is often spread over several households, and it is sometimes difficult to discover the true source. They can easily be transported in furniture when people move house, and one has to be very careful if one is bringing into the house packages which have been stored for long in a food store or which have come from tropical countries.

Fleas and lice

See pages 28–31. You only need to start talking about fleas or lice and soon everyone will be scratching themselves. They immediately think of the human flea or the cat and dog fleas, which sometimes attack humans. In fact there are over 1300 species of flea known, including about 50 found in this country.

You can pick up a flea anywhere where there is a crowd, though these days they are nothing like as common as they used to be.

If you are unlucky enough to pick up a flea just before you go on your summer holiday (and fleas are most active in the summer) the flea may lay its eggs in your house. Although the adults live on blood, the larvae do not. They live on all kinds of offal and rubbish under the skirting boards. By the time you return from holiday the larvae will have become adults and you may be literally jumped on by a horde of starving fleas.

A dog or cat may also pick up fleas in the absence of its owners, and they can multiply rapidly. Although these fleas do not normally attack humans, they will do so if they are starving—and the flea population may have grown too big for one pet to support.

Ordinary fleas are not dangerous. On the other hand rat fleas, especially the flea of the black rat, can transmit killing diseases.

Lice used to be common. Just after 1945 they became much less common but now they are coming back again. Having lice used to be thought quite usual. In one Swedish village a louse was used to choose the new mayor. All the candidates sat round a table with their beards outstretched. A louse was released in the middle of the table, and the person whose beard attracted the louse became the new mayor.

Lice are not just parasites on the poor. When gentlemen wore pigtails it was quite common even for noblemen to have lice, and they carried special little scratchers to combat them. Even the fur collar round the neck of a coat was once a form of lice control. Body lice were attracted to this kind of fur collar and in the Middle Ages, when enough lice had gathered, the collar, and the lice, were dipped in boiling water.

Gnats and flies

See pages 30–34. These are among the commonest indoor pests from early spring to late autumn.

The common gnat, *Culex pipiens*, is our best known gnat, and also the most troublesome. It emerges only at dusk, hiding during the day on the ceiling, behind pictures and in other dark places. The males live on plant juices, while the females need warm blood in order to produce fertile eggs.

The eggs are usually laid in water, though sometimes in damp soil. The larvae live in the water for some time, pupate, and only begin to suck blood when they are adults.

What attracts gnats to us? Almost certainly we exude some chemical which attracts them, but we do not yet know what it is exactly. We do know that a sweaty skin attracts them more than a dry one.

The common gnat is no more than a nuisance, but several other kinds of mosquito can transmit disease. In the tropics malaria and yellow fever are both spread by mosquitoes. The malaria mosquito, *Anopheles maculipennis,* is found in Britain too, but malaria is not common here. Only if the mosquito has bitten a malaria patient can it transmit the disease.

The house fly is the most familiar of the many kinds of fly found in Britain. Most people know that it is a 'dirty' animal but few understand the real danger. House flies can spread typhoid and paratyphoid with their droppings, as well as dysentry, and they can also play a dangerous part once a cholera epidemic has started.

Like rats, house flies live wherever man lives. The female fly lives from two to three months and lays between 600 and 3000 eggs, in manure or rotting food and preferably in damp places.

Bees and wasps
See pages 34–35. Although bees can sting painfully, few people seem to be afraid of them. A single bee getting into the house can usually be gently pushed out again. If a swarm enters, then telephoning a local bee-keeper is the best answer.

Wasps can be more of a nuisance, because they can build a nest inside the house, between ceilings, under floors, in chimneys or in air vents. When this happens, the wasps are bound to look for food inside the house as well as outside, and there is usually plenty for them. They eat crumbs which have been dropped as well as the remains of sugar or sugary liquid in empty cups and lemonade glasses.

Wasps are more aggressive than bees, and will not always allow themselves to be driven away. Sometimes they will counter-attack.

It is not easy to remove a wasps' nest, and it is a job to be left to the experts. They must first find how many exits there are from the nest—usually two. Then the technique is to wait until dusk, when all the wasps are in the nest, plug one of the holes with paper or cloth, and then squirt a powerful insecticide into the other hole. It takes some time for the insecticide to reach the far corners of the nest, so a long squirt is needed.

Wasps can also be a nuisance when you are camping or picnicking. The simplest solution here is to place a jam jar with a little jam in it at some distance from the picnic. The wasps will soon find this and settle to feed on it.

Ants
See pages 36–37. Ants inside the house can develop into a real plague. Black ants never

Black ants—workers and winged queens

settle in the house preferring tiles or flat stones in the garden which keep the heat long after sunset. But they will certainly raid the house for food, and in really bad cases it is impossible to open a sugar pot or jam jar without finding an ant in it.

They are not dirty animals—in fact they are extremely clean—but we would prefer to be without them nonetheless. The way to get rid of them is to find the nest, which is not hard. You can usually see cracks between tiles or in concrete and these cracks are the entrances to the nest, with ants walking busily in and out. If you can lift the tile or slab of paving, you will find a large number of ants under it; as soon as you disturb them they will pick up white objects, which are the pupæ, and try to get to the nest which is deeper down still. It is enough to sprinkle a few spoonfuls of insect powder around this area.

Ants demonstrate the truth of the old proverb 'Many a little makes a muckle.' Both the black ants and the newcomer, the pharaoh's ant can cause a real plague, although each is no more than a few millimetres long.

Spiders and spider-like animals

See page 39. Most spiders do more good than harm, and it is as well to leave them alone as far as possible, and to put up with cobwebs in cellars and attics.

Mites or ticks, however, can be a real nuisance, especially when they choose humans or pets as their hosts.

In the last few years a new pest has made itself felt in cities, because of the large number of pigeons which live in towns. Pigeons soil buildings and statues, as well as the washing on clothes lines, with their droppings, but this is a minor point. They take all the available food and nesting sites, so other birds are decreasing in numbers. The pigeon can transmit several diseases such as psittacosis, paratyphoid, and a form of fowl-pest which affects humans. Pigeons are often covered with mites, and when the young birds leave the nests, the mites enter houses in search of a new host. They gorge themselves on human blood, causing a rash on some people.

How should we deal with pests?

We could conclude that pests are a great danger to man's health, and also to his possessions including food, and that we have little choice but to fight vigorously against them. On the other hand we must be careful that we do not injure ourselves in the process, by using poisons wrongly, and also that we do not cause a plague of one animal by completely wiping out another which we regard as a pest.

Other books

Because pests are an unpleasant subject, there are not many books about them. You might find the following books useful in studying insects:

Insects in colour, ND Riley (Blandford)
Name this insect, EF Daglish (Dent)
The insect world, SA Manning (World's Work)
Ants from close up, LH Newman (Cassell)
Insect life, MJD Hirons (Blandford)
The world of an insect, R Chauvin (World University Library)
Fleas—their intricate lives and plaguey history, H Hoke and V Pitt (Franklin Watts)
Rats and mice, Ralph Whitlock (Wayland)

Jack Black, Rat Catcher to Her Majesty Queen Victoria, in his special uniform

Index of Latin names

All the numbers in this index refer to pages, not to picture numbers.

Index

All numbers refer to pages, not to illustration numbers.